A Word to Parents

This book grew out of a desire to provide a companion study journal for children for use alongside the David: His Story Is Our Story adult study journal.

Love God Greatly is dedicated to making God's Word available to our beautiful community of women... and now, women have the opportunity to share God's Word with children through this study uniquely crafted for young hearts. Please note that the verses listed in this journal are the exact same verses listed in the adult journal. While that is perfectly fine for almost everyday, there are a few days when you may want your child to read and write out a different verse due to more adult content. Please feel the freedom to adjust the Scripture passage reading any day if you deem necessary.

The Intro to David for Kids (pg. 4) may assist you in preparing your child for the weeks ahead. We are excited about this new resource that offers God's Word to the next generation of believers, and we praise God that you are a part of this adventure!

Table of contents

INTRO TO DAVID: HIS STORY IS OUR STORY

The Story of David

Have you ever wondered if God could really use someone like you? Then the story of David is for you. The shepherd. The king. The warrior. The friend. The sinner. The man of faith. David is known for carrying many titles over the span of his lifetime, but he is most often referred to as a man after God's own heart. While David's transparent faith was true and his loyalty to his Lord was real, an in-depth look into Scripture reveals that his life was also marked by times of drama, deceit, devastation, and doubt. How then is David known for being such an influential Bible hero? Unfaithful David served a faithful God.

In this eight-week Love God Greatly Bible study, our look into the life of David will ultimately point us to a better Shepherd, Friend, and King: Jesus. On Mondays and Tuesdays of each week we'll explore David's life. Wednesdays and Thursdays we will look at Jesus, and Fridays we'll examine our own hearts. As we study together, see if you can spot God's faithfulness, His kindness, His patience, His justice, His mercy, and His grace in the life of David. For the God of David is our God as well.

The life God chose for David truly was a life of adventure rooted in faith….I wonder what kind of amazing adventures God has planned for your life? Remember, you are never too young to do mighty things for God! Through the power of Christ in us, you too can become a child after God's own heart.

Let's get started!!!!!

Goals

We believe it's important to write out goals for each session. Take some time now and write three goals you would like to focus on this session as we begin to rise each day and dig into God's Word. Make sure and refer back to these goals throughout the next eight weeks to help you stay focused. YOU CAN DO IT!!!

My goals for this session are:

1.

2.

3.

Signature: _____

Date: _____

Reading Plan

		Read	SOAP
WEEK 1	Monday	1 Samuel 16: 1-12; Psalm 78:70-72	Psalm 78:70-72
	Tuesday	1 Sam 17: 12-15; 32-37	1 Sam 17:14,15
	Wednesday	Ezekiel 34:15-31	Ezekiel 34:15–16, 31
	Thursday	Isaiah 40:9-11	Isaiah 40:10-11
	Friday	Psalm 100	Psalm 100:3
	Response Day		
WEEK 2	Monday	2 Sam. 5:1-5, 9-12	2 Sam. 5:10
	Tuesday	2 Samuel 7:8,9,16	2 Samuel 7:16
	Wednesday	John 18:33-37	John 18:36
	Thursday	Isaiah 9:6-7	Isaiah 9:7
	Friday	Romans 8:17; Ephesians 2:19	Ephesians 2:19
	Response Day		
WEEK 3	Monday	1 Samuel 21:10-13	1 Samuel 21: 12-13
	Tuesday	2 Samuel 12:1-17	2 Samuel 12:16-17
	Wednesday	John 1-4, 14	John 1:14
	Thursday	Hebrews 2:14-18	hebrews 2:17-18
	Friday	John 15:5; 2 Corinthians 12:9	2 Corinthians 12:9
	Response Day		
WEEK 4	Monday	1 Samuel 18:6-16	1 Samuel 18:14
	Tuesday	Psalm 144: 1-4	Psalm 144:1
	Wednesday	Revelation 19:11-16	Revelation 19:11
	Thursday	Psalm 24	Psalm 24: 8
	Friday	Ephesians 6:10-18	Ephesians 6:10-13
	Response Day		
WEEK 5	Monday	1 Samuel 18:1-5; 20:42; 23:16-18	1 Samuel 20:42
	Tuesday	2 Samuel 1:1-27	2 Samuel 1:26
	Wednesday	John 15:13-17	John 15:15
	Thursday	Proverbs 17:17; Proverbs 18:24	Proverbs 17:17
	Friday	Ephesians 4:29-32	Ephesians 4:32
	Response Day		
WEEK 6	Monday	2 Samuel 11:1–27	2 Samuel 11:27
	Tuesday	2 Samuel 12:1–15	2 Samuel 12:13-15
	Wednesday	1 Timothy 1:12-16	1 Timothy 1:15
	Thursday	Genesis 8:21; 1 John 1:8-9	1 John 1:8-9
	Friday	Acts 3:19	Acts 3:19
	Response Day		
WEEK 7	Monday	Acts 13:22	Acts 13:22
	Tuesday	1 Samuel 13: 8-15	1 Samuel 13:14
	Wednesday	Matthew 17:1-7	Matthew 17:5
	Thursday	Matthew 10:29-31	Matthew 10:29-31
	Friday	1 Peter 2:9-10	1 Peter 2:9
	Response Day		
WEEK 8	Monday	1 Samuel 17:33-47	1 Samuel 17:45
	Tuesday	Psalm 27	Psalm 27:1
	Wednesday	2 Thessalonians 3:1-5	2 Thessalonians 3:3-5
	Thursday	Jeremiah 17:7-8	Jeremiah 17:7-8
	Friday	Hebrews 10:19-25	Hebrews 10:21-23
	Response Day		

Week 1

Prayer focus for this week: Spend time praying for your family members.

	Praying	Praise
Monday		
Tuesday		
Wednesday		
Thursday		
Friday		

KNOW THAT THE LORD, HE IS GOD! IT IS HE WHO MADE US, AND WE ARE HIS; WE ARE HIS PEOPLE, AND THE SHEEP OF HIS PASTURE.

Psalm 100:3 (ESV)

Scripture for Week 1

DAVID THE SHEPHERD BOY

MONDAY   *1 SAMUEL 16:1-12 (ESV)*

¹⁶ The Lord said to Samuel, "How long will you grieve over Saul, since I have rejected him from being king over Israel? Fill your horn with oil, and go. I will send you to Jesse the Bethlehemite, for I have provided for myself a king among his sons." ² And Samuel said, "How can I go? If Saul hears it, he will kill me." And the Lord said, "Take a heifer with you and say, 'I have come to sacrifice to the Lord.' ³ And invite Jesse to the sacrifice, and I will show you what you shall do. And you shall anoint for me him whom I declare to you."⁴ Samuel did what the Lord commanded and came to Bethlehem. The elders of the city came to meet him trembling and said, "Do you come peaceably?" ⁵ And he said, "Peaceably; I have come to sacrifice to the Lord. Consecrate yourselves, and come with me to the sacrifice." And he consecrated Jesse and his sons and invited them to the sacrifice.

⁶ When they came, he looked on Eliab and thought, "Surely the Lord's anointed is before him." ⁷ But the Lord said to Samuel, "Do not look on his appearance or on the height of his stature, because I have rejected him. For the Lord sees not as man sees: man looks on the outward appearance, but the Lord looks on the heart." ⁸ Then Jesse called Abinadab and made him pass before Samuel. And he said, "Neither has the Lord chosen this one." ⁹ Then Jesse made Shammah pass by. And he said, "Neither has the Lord chosen this one." ¹⁰ And Jesse made seven of his sons pass before Samuel. And Samuel said to Jesse, "The Lord has not chosen these." ¹¹ Then Samuel said to Jesse, "Are all your sons here?" And he said, "There remains yet the youngest, but behold, he is keeping the sheep." And Samuel said to Jesse, "Send and get him, for we will not sit down till he comes here." ¹² And he sent and brought him in. Now he was ruddy and had beautiful eyes and was handsome. And the Lord said, "Arise, anoint him, for this is he."

PSALM 78:70-72 (ESV)

⁷⁰ He chose David his servant
   and took him from the sheepfolds;
⁷¹ from following the nursing ewes he brought him
   to shepherd Jacob his people,
   Israel his inheritance.
⁷² With upright heart he shepherded them
   and guided them with his skillful hand.

[12] Now David was the son of an Ephrathite of Bethlehem in Judah, named Jesse, who had eight sons. In the days of Saul the man was already old and advanced in years. [13] The three oldest sons of Jesse had followed Saul to the battle. And the names of his three sons who went to the battle were Eliab the firstborn, and next to him Abinadab, and the third Shammah. [14] David was the youngest. The three eldest followed Saul, [15] but David went back and forth from Saul to feed his father's sheep at Bethlehem.

[32] And David said to Saul, "Let no man's heart fail because of him. Your servant will go and fight with this Philistine." [33] And Saul said to David, "You are not able to go against this Philistine to fight with him, for you are but a youth, and he has been a man of war from his youth." [34] But David said to Saul, "Your servant used to keep sheep for his father. And when there came a lion, or a bear, and took a lamb from the flock, [35] I went after him and struck him and delivered it out of his mouth. And if he arose against me, I caught him by his beard and struck him and killed him. [36] Your servant has struck down both lions and bears, and this uncircumcised Philistine shall be like one of them, for he has defied the armies of the living God." [37] And David said, "The Lord who delivered me from the paw of the lion and from the paw of the bear will deliver me from the hand of this Philistine." And Saul said to David, "Go, and the Lord be with you!"

Scripture for Week 1

WEDNESDAY - GOD THE BETTER SHEPHERD   *EZEKIEL 34:15-31 (ESV)*

[15] I myself will be the shepherd of my sheep, and I myself will make them lie down, declares the Lord God. [16] I will seek the lost, and I will bring back the strayed, and I will bind up the injured, and I will strengthen the weak, and the fat and the strong I will destroy. I will feed them in justice. [17] "As for you, my flock, thus says the Lord God: Behold, I judge between sheep and sheep, between rams and male goats. [18] Is it not enough for you to feed on the good pasture, that you must tread down with your feet the rest of your pasture; and to drink of clear water, that you must muddy the rest of the water with your feet? [19] And must my sheep eat what you have trodden with your feet, and drink what you have muddied with your feet?

[20] "Therefore, thus says the Lord God to them: Behold, I, I myself will judge between the fat sheep and the lean sheep. [21] Because you push with side and shoulder, and thrust at all the weak with your horns, till you have scattered them abroad, [22] I will rescue my flock; they shall no longer be a prey. And I will judge between sheep and sheep. [23] And I will set up over them one shepherd, my servant David, and he shall feed them: he shall feed them and be their shepherd. [24] And I, the Lord, will be their God, and my servant David shall be prince among them. I am the Lord; I have spoken.

[25] "I will make with them a covenant of peace and banish wild beasts from the land, so that they may dwell securely in the wilderness and sleep in the woods. [26] And I will make them and the places all around my hill a blessing, and I will send down the showers in their season; they shall be showers of blessing. [27] And the trees of the field shall yield their fruit, and the earth shall yield its increase, and they shall be secure in their land. And they shall know that I am the Lord, when I break the bars of their yoke, and deliver them from the hand of those who enslaved them. [28] They shall no more be a prey to the nations, nor shall the beasts of the land devour them. They shall dwell securely, and none shall make them afraid. [29] And I will provide for them renowned plantations so that they shall no more be consumed with hunger in the land, and no longer suffer the reproach of the nations. [30] And they shall know that I am the Lord their God with them, and that they, the house of Israel, are my people, declares the Lord God. [31] And you are my sheep, human sheep of my pasture, and I am your God, declares the Lord God."

THURSDAY

[9] Go on up to a high mountain,
    O Zion, herald of good news;
lift up your voice with strength,
    O Jerusalem, herald of good news;
    lift it up, fear not;
say to the cities of Judah,
    "Behold your God!"
[10] Behold, the Lord God comes with might,
    and his arm rules for him;
behold, his reward is with him,
    and his recompense before him.
[11] He will tend his flock like a shepherd;
    he will gather the lambs in his arms;
he will carry them in his bosom,
    and gently lead those that are with young.

FRIDAY

PSALM 100 (ESV)

Make a joyful noise to the Lord, all the earth!
[2]   Serve the Lord with gladness!
    Come into his presence with singing!
[3] Know that the Lord, he is God!
    It is he who made us, and we are his;
    we are his people, and the sheep of his pasture.
[4] Enter his gates with thanksgiving,
    and his courts with praise!
    Give thanks to him; bless his name!
[5] For the Lord is good;
    his steadfast love endures forever,
    and his faithfulness to all generations.

Monday

READ: 1 Samuel 16:1-12; Psalm 78:70-72   **WRITE**: Psalm 78:70-72

1. Write out today's **SCRIPTURE** passage.

_____

_____

_____

_____

_____

_____

_____

_____

_____

2. On the blank page to the right, **DRAW** or **WRITE** what this passage means to you.

3. My **PRAYER** for today:

_____

_____

_____

_____

_____

Monday

Tuesday

READ: 1 Samuel 17:12-15; 32-37   WRITE: 1 Samuel 17:14,15

1. Write out today's **SCRIPTURE** passage.

_____

_____

_____

_____

_____

_____

_____

_____

_____

_____

2. On the blank page to the right, **DRAW** or **WRITE** what this passage means to you.

3. My **PRAYER** for today:

_____

_____

_____

_____

_____

Tuesday

Wednesday

READ: Ezekiel 34:15-31   WRITE: Ezekiel 34:15–16, 31

1. Write out today's **SCRIPTURE** passage.

_____

_____

_____

_____

_____

_____

_____

_____

_____

_____

2. On the blank page to the right, **DRAW** or **WRITE** what this passage means to you.

3. My **PRAYER** for today:

_____

_____

_____

_____

_____

Wednesday

Thursday

READ: Isaiah 40:9-11   WRITE: Isaiah 40:10-11

1. Write out today's **SCRIPTURE** passage.

_____

_____

_____

_____

_____

_____

_____

_____

2. On the blank page to the right, **DRAW** or **WRITE** what this passage means to you.

3. My **PRAYER** for today:

_____

_____

_____

_____

Thursday

Friday

READ: Psalm 100   **WRITE:** Psalm 100:3

1. Write out today's **SCRIPTURE** passage.

_____

_____

_____

_____

_____

_____

_____

_____

_____

2. On the blank page to the right, **DRAW** or **WRITE** what this passage means to you.

3. My **PRAYER** for today:

_____

_____

_____

_____

_____

Friday

This week I learned...

Use the space below to draw a picture or write about what you learned this week from your time in God's Word.

Week 2

Prayer focus for this week: Spend time praying for your country.

	Praying	Praise
Monday		
Tuesday		
Wednesday		
Thursday		
Friday		

AND DAVID BECAME GREATER AND GREATER, FOR THE LORD, THE GOD OF HOSTS, WAS WITH HIM.

2 Samuel 5:10 (ESV)

Scripture for Week 2

DAVID THE KING

MONDAY *2 SAMUEL 5:1-5, 9-12 (ESV)*

⁵ Then all the tribes of Israel came to David at Hebron and said, "Behold, we are your bone and flesh. ² In times past, when Saul was king over us, it was you who led out and brought in Israel. And the Lord said to you, 'You shall be shepherd of my people Israel, and you shall be prince over Israel.'" ³ So all the elders of Israel came to the king at Hebron, and King David made a covenant with them at Hebron before the Lord, and they anointed David king over Israel. ⁴ David was thirty years old when he began to reign, and he reigned forty years. ⁵ At Hebron he reigned over Judah seven years and six months, and at Jerusalem he reigned over all Israel and Judah thirty-three years.

⁹ And David lived in the stronghold and called it the city of David. And David built the city all around from the Millo inward. ¹⁰ And David became greater and greater, for the Lord, the God of hosts, was with him.

¹¹ And Hiram king of Tyre sent messengers to David, and cedar trees, also carpenters and masons who built David a house. ¹² And David knew that the Lord had established him king over Israel, and that he had exalted his kingdom for the sake of his people Israel.

TUESDAY *2 SAMUEL 7:8, 9, 16 (ESV)*

⁸ Now, therefore, thus you shall say to my servant David, 'Thus says the Lord of hosts, I took you from the pasture, from following the sheep, that you should be prince over my people Israel.

⁹ And I have been with you wherever you went and have cut off all your enemies from before you. And I will make for you a great name, like the name of the great ones of the earth.

¹⁶ And your house and your kingdom shall be made sure forever before me. Your throne shall be established forever.'"

WEDNESDAY - JESUS THE BETTER KING   JOHN 18:33-37 (ESV)

[33] So Pilate entered his headquarters again and called Jesus and said to him, "Are you the King of the Jews?" [34] Jesus answered, "Do you say this of your own accord, or did others say it to you about me?" [35] Pilate answered, "Am I a Jew? Your own nation and the chief priests have delivered you over to me. What have you done?" [36] Jesus answered, "My kingdom is not of this world. If my kingdom were of this world, my servants would have been fighting, that I might not be delivered over to the Jews. But my kingdom is not from the world." [37] Then Pilate said to him, "So you are a king?" Jesus answered, "You say that I am a king. For this purpose I was born and for this purpose I have come into the world—to bear witness to the truth. Everyone who is of the truth listens to my voice."

THURSDAY   ISAIAH 9:6-7 (ESV)

[6] For to us a child is born,
　　to us a son is given;
and the government shall be upon his shoulder,
　　and his name shall be called
Wonderful Counselor, Mighty God,
　　Everlasting Father, Prince of Peace.
[7] Of the increase of his government and of peace
　　there will be no end,
on the throne of David and over his kingdom,
　　to establish it and to uphold it
with justice and with righteousness
　　from this time forth and forevermore.
The zeal of the Lord of hosts will do this.

FRIDAY   ROMANS 8:17 (ESV)

[17] and if children, then heirs—heirs of God and fellow heirs with Christ, provided we suffer with him in order that we may also be glorified with him.

EPHESIANS 2:19 (ESV)

[19] So then you are no longer strangers and aliens, but you are fellow citizens with the saints and members of the household of God

Monday

READ: 2 Samuel 5:1-5, 9-12   **WRITE:** 2 Samuel 5:10

1. Write out today's **SCRIPTURE** passage.

_____

_____

_____

_____

_____

_____

_____

_____

_____

_____

2. On the blank page to the right, **DRAW** or **WRITE** what this passage means to you.

3. My **PRAYER** for today:

_____

_____

_____

_____

Monday

Tuesday

READ: 2 Samuel 7:8, 9, 16   WRITE: 2 Samuel 7:16

1. Write out today's SCRIPTURE passage.

_____

_____

_____

_____

_____

_____

_____

_____

_____

2. On the blank page to the right, DRAW or WRITE what this passage means to you.

3. My PRAYER for today:

_____

_____

_____

_____

Tuesday

Wednesday

READ: John 18:33-37   WRITE: John 18:36

1. Write out today's **SCRIPTURE** passage.

_____

_____

_____

_____

_____

_____

_____

_____

_____

2. On the blank page to the right, **DRAW** or **WRITE** what this passage means to you.

3. My **PRAYER** for today:

_____

_____

_____

_____

Wednesday

READ: Isaiah 9:6-7   WRITE: Isaiah 9:7

1. Write out today's **SCRIPTURE** passage.

_____

_____

_____

_____

_____

_____

_____

_____

_____

_____

2. On the blank page to the right, **DRAW** or **WRITE** what this passage means to you.

3. My **PRAYER** for today:

_____

_____

_____

_____

_____

Thursday

Friday

READ: Romans 8:17; Ephesians 2:19   **WRITE**: Ephesians 2:19

1. Write out today's **SCRIPTURE** passage.

_____

_____

_____

_____

_____

_____

_____

_____

_____

_____

2. On the blank page to the right, **DRAW** or **WRITE** what this passage means to you.

3. My **PRAYER** for today:

_____

_____

_____

_____

_____

Friday

This week I learned...

Use the space below to draw a picture or write about what you learned this week from your time in God's Word.

Week 3

Prayer focus for this week: Spend time praying for your friends.

	Praying	Praise
Monday		
Tuesday		
Wednesday		
Thursday		
Friday		

BUT HE SAID TO ME, "MY GRACE IS SUFFICIENT FOR YOU, FOR MY POWER IS MADE PERFECT IN WEAKNESS." THEREFORE I WILL BOAST ALL THE MORE GLADLY OF MY WEAKNESSES, SO THAT THE POWER OF CHRIST MAY REST UPON ME.

2 Corinthians 12:9 (ESV)

Scripture for Week 3

DAVID THE MAN

MONDAY   *1 SAMUEL 21:10-13 (ESV)*

¹⁰ And David rose and fled that day from Saul and went to Achish the king of Gath. ¹¹ And the servants of Achish said to him, "Is not this David the king of the land? Did they not sing to one another of him in dances,

'Saul has struck down his thousands,

and David his ten thousands'?"

¹² And David took these words to heart and was much afraid of Achish the king of Gath.¹³ So he changed his behavior before them and pretended to be insane in their hands and made marks on the doors of the gate and let his spittle run down his beard.

TUESDAY   *2 SAMUEL 12:1-17 (ESV)*

¹² And the Lord sent Nathan to David. He came to him and said to him, "There were two men in a certain city, the one rich and the other poor. ² The rich man had very many flocks and herds, ³ but the poor man had nothing but one little ewe lamb, which he had bought. And he brought it up, and it grew up with him and with his children. It used to eat of his morsel and drink from his cup and lie in his arms, and it was like a daughter to him. ⁴ Now there came a traveler to the rich man, and he was unwilling to take one of his own flock or herd to prepare for the guest who had come to him, but he took the poor man's lamb and prepared it for the man who had come to him." ⁵ Then David's anger was greatly kindled against the man, and he said to Nathan, "As the Lord lives, the man who has done this deserves to die, ⁶ and he shall restore the lamb fourfold, because he did this thing, and because he had no pity."

⁷ Nathan said to David, "You are the man! Thus says the Lord, the God of Israel, 'I anointed you king over Israel, and I delivered you out of the hand of Saul. ⁸ And I gave you your master's house and your master's wives into your arms and gave you the house of Israel and of Judah. And if this were too little, I would add to you as much more. ⁹ Why have you despised the word of the Lord, to do what is evil in his sight? You have struck down Uriah the Hittite with the sword and have taken his wife to be your wife and have killed him with the sword of the Ammonites. ¹⁰ Now therefore the sword shall never depart from your house, because you have despised me and have taken the wife of Uriah the Hittite to be your wife.' ¹¹ Thus says the Lord, 'Behold, I will raise up evil against you out of your own house. And I will take your wives before your eyes and give them to your

neighbor, and he shall lie with your wives in the sight of this sun. ¹² For you did it secretly, but I will do this thing before all Israel and before the sun.'" ¹³ David said to Nathan, "I have sinned against the Lord." And Nathan said to David, "The Lord also has put away your sin; you shall not die. ¹⁴ Nevertheless, because by this deed you have utterly scorned the Lord, the child who is born to you shall die." ¹⁵ Then Nathan went to his house.

And the Lord afflicted the child that Uriah's wife bore to David, and he became sick.¹⁶ David therefore sought God on behalf of the child. And David fasted and went in and lay all night on the ground. ¹⁷ And the elders of his house stood beside him, to raise him from the ground, but he would not, nor did he eat food with them.

WEDNESDAY - JESUS THE BETTER MAN   *JOHN 1:1-4, 14 (ESV)*

¹ In the beginning was the Word, and the Word was with God, and the Word was God.² He was in the beginning with God. ³ All things were made through him, and without him was not any thing made that was made. ⁴ In him was life, and the life was the light of men.

¹⁴ And the Word became flesh and dwelt among us, and we have seen his glory, glory as of the only Son from the Father, full of grace and truth.

THURSDAY   *HEBREWS 2:14-18 (ESV)*

¹⁴ Since therefore the children share in flesh and blood, he himself likewise partook of the same things, that through death he might destroy the one who has the power of death, that is, the devil, ¹⁵ and deliver all those who through fear of death were subject to lifelong slavery. ¹⁶ For surely it is not angels that he helps, but he helps the offspring of Abraham.¹⁷ Therefore he had to be made like his brothers in every respect, so that he might become a merciful and faithful high priest in the service of God, to make propitiation for the sins of the people. ¹⁸ For because he himself has suffered when tempted, he is able to help those who are being tempted.

FRIDAY   *JOHN 15:5 (ESV)*

⁵ I am the vine; you are the branches. Whoever abides in me and I in him, he it is that bears much fruit, for apart from me you can do nothing.

2 CORINTHIANS 12:9 (ESV)

⁹ But he said to me, "My grace is sufficient for you, for my power is made perfect in weakness." Therefore I will boast all the more gladly of my weaknesses, so that the power of Christ may rest upon me.

Monday

READ: 1 Samuel 21:10-13   **WRITE:** 1 Samuel 21:12-13

1. Write out today's **SCRIPTURE** passage.

_____

_____

_____

_____

_____

_____

_____

_____

_____

2. On the blank page to the right, **DRAW** or **WRITE** what this passage means to you.

3. My **PRAYER** for today:

_____

_____

_____

_____

Monday

Tuesday

READ: 2 Samuel 12:1-17   **WRITE:** 2 Samuel 12:16-17

1. Write out today's **SCRIPTURE** passage.

_____

_____

_____

_____

_____

_____

_____

_____

_____

_____

2. On the blank page to the right, **DRAW** or **WRITE** what this passage means to you.

3. My **PRAYER** for today:

_____

_____

_____

_____

_____

Tuesday

Wednesday

READ: John 1:1-4, 14　　　　　　　　**WRITE**: John 1:14

1. Write out today's **SCRIPTURE** passage.

_____

_____

_____

_____

_____

_____

_____

_____

_____

2. On the blank page to the right, **DRAW** or **WRITE** what this passage means to you.

3. My **PRAYER** for today:

_____

_____

_____

_____

_____

Wednesday

Thursday

READ: Hebrews 2:14-18   WRITE: Hebrews 2:17-18

1. Write out today's **SCRIPTURE** passage.

_____

_____

_____

_____

_____

_____

_____

_____

_____

_____

2. On the blank page to the right, **DRAW** or **WRITE** what this passage means to you.

3. My **PRAYER** for today:

_____

_____

_____

_____

_____

Thursday

Friday

1. Write out today's **SCRIPTURE** passage.

_____

_____

_____

_____

_____

_____

_____

_____

_____

_____

2. On the blank page to the right, **DRAW** or **WRITE** what this passage means to you.

3. My **PRAYER** for today:

_____

_____

_____

_____

_____

Friday

This week I learned...

Use the space below to draw a picture or write about what you learned this week from your time in God's Word.

Week 4

Prayer focus for this week: Spend time praying for your church.

	Praying	Praise
Monday		
Tuesday		
Wednesday		
Thursday		
Friday		

Scripture for Week 4

DAVID THE WARRIOR

MONDAY   *1 SAMUEL 18:6-16 (ESV)*

⁶ As they were coming home, when David returned from striking down the Philistine, the women came out of all the cities of Israel, singing and dancing, to meet King Saul, with tambourines, with songs of joy, and with musical instruments. ⁷ And the women sang to one another as they celebrated,

"Saul has struck down his thousands,

and David his ten thousands."

⁸ And Saul was very angry, and this saying displeased him. He said, "They have ascribed to David ten thousands, and to me they have ascribed thousands, and what more can he have but the kingdom?" ⁹ And Saul eyed David from that day on.

¹⁰ The next day a harmful spirit from God rushed upon Saul, and he raved within his house while David was playing the lyre, as he did day by day. Saul had his spear in his hand. ¹¹ And Saul hurled the spear, for he thought, "I will pin David to the wall." But David evaded him twice.

¹² Saul was afraid of David because the Lord was with him but had departed from Saul.¹³ So Saul removed him from his presence and made him a commander of a thousand.And he went out and came in before the people. ¹⁴ And David had success in all his undertakings, for the Lord was with him. ¹⁵ And when Saul saw that he had great success, he stood in fearful awe of him. ¹⁶ But all Israel and Judah loved David, for he went out and came in before them.

TUESDAY   *PSALM 144:1-4 (ESV)*

Blessed be the Lord, my rock,
    who trains my hands for war,
    and my fingers for battle;
² he is my steadfast love and my fortress,
    my stronghold and my deliverer,
my shield and he in whom I take refuge,
    who subdues peoples under me.
³ O Lord, what is man that you regard him,
    or the son of man that you think of him?
⁴ Man is like a breath;
    his days are like a passing shadow.

WEDNESDAY - JESUS THE BETTER WARRIOR   *REVELATION 19:11-16 (ESV)*

¹¹ Then I saw heaven opened, and behold, a white horse! The one sitting on it is called Faithful and True, and in righteousness he judges and makes war. ¹² His eyes are like a flame of fire, and on his head are many diadems, and he has a name written that no one knows but himself. ¹³ He is clothed in a robe dipped in blood, and the name by which he is called is The Word of God. ¹⁴ And the armies of heaven, arrayed in fine linen, white and pure, were following him on white horses. ¹⁵ From his mouth comes a sharp sword with which to strike down the nations, and he will rule them with a rod of iron. He will tread the winepress of the fury of the wrath of God the Almighty. ¹⁶ On his robe and on his thigh he has a name written, King of kings and Lord of lords.

Scripture for Week 4

THURSDAY   *PSALM 24 (ESV)*

The earth is the Lord's and the fullness thereof,
  the world and those who dwell therein,
² for he has founded it upon the seas
  and established it upon the rivers.
³ Who shall ascend the hill of the Lord?
  And who shall stand in his holy place?
⁴ He who has clean hands and a pure heart,
  who does not lift up his soul to what is false
  and does not swear deceitfully.
⁵ He will receive blessing from the Lord
  and righteousness from the God of his salvation.
⁶ Such is the generation of those who seek him,
  who seek the face of the God of Jacob. *Selah*
⁷ Lift up your heads, O gates!
  And be lifted up, O ancient doors,
  that the King of glory may come in.
⁸ Who is this King of glory?
  The Lord, strong and mighty,
  the Lord, mighty in battle!
⁹ Lift up your heads, O gates!
  And lift them up, O ancient doors,
  that the King of glory may come in.
¹⁰ Who is this King of glory?
  The Lord of hosts,
  he is the King of glory! *Selah*

[10] Finally, be strong in the Lord and in the strength of his might. [11] Put on the whole armor of God, that you may be able to stand against the schemes of the devil. [12] For we do not wrestle against flesh and blood, but against the rulers, against the authorities, against the cosmic powers over this present darkness, against the spiritual forces of evil in the heavenly places. [13] Therefore take up the whole armor of God, that you may be able to withstand in the evil day, and having done all, to stand firm. [14] Stand therefore, having fastened on the belt of truth, and having put on the breastplate of righteousness, [15] and,as shoes for your feet, having put on the readiness given by the gospel of peace. [16] In all circumstances take up the shield of faith, with which you can extinguish all the flaming darts of the evil one; [17] and take the helmet of salvation, and the sword of the Spirit, which is the word of God, [18] praying at all times in the Spirit, with all prayer and supplication. To that end keep alert with all perseverance, making supplication for all the saints

Monday

1. Write out today's **SCRIPTURE** passage.

_____

_____

_____

_____

_____

_____

_____

_____

_____

_____

2. On the blank page to the right, **DRAW** or **WRITE** what this passage means to you.

3. My **PRAYER** for today:

_____

_____

_____

_____

_____

Monday

READ: Psalm 144: 1-4   WRITE: Psalm 144:1

1. Write out today's **SCRIPTURE** passage.

_____

_____

_____

_____

_____

_____

_____

_____

_____

2. On the blank page to the right, **DRAW** or **WRITE** what this passage means to you.

3. My **PRAYER** for today:

_____

_____

_____

_____

_____

Tuesday

Wednesday

READ: Revelation 19:11-16

WRITE: Revelation 19:11

1. Write out today's SCRIPTURE passage.

_____

_____

_____

_____

_____

_____

_____

_____

_____

_____

2. On the blank page to the right, DRAW or WRITE what this passage means to you.

3. My PRAYER for today:

_____

_____

_____

_____

_____

Wednesday

READ: Psalm 24   **WRITE:** Psalm 24: 8

1. Write out today's **SCRIPTURE** passage.

_____

_____

_____

_____

_____

_____

_____

_____

_____

_____

2. On the blank page to the right, **DRAW** or **WRITE** what this passage means to you.

3. My **PRAYER** for today:

_____

_____

_____

_____

_____

_____

Thursday

Friday

READ: Ephesians 6:10-18   **WRITE**: Ephesians 6:10-13

1. Write out today's **SCRIPTURE** passage.

_____

_____

_____

_____

_____

_____

_____

_____

_____

_____

2. On the blank page to the right, **DRAW** or **WRITE** what this passage means to you.

3. My **PRAYER** for today:

_____

_____

_____

_____

_____

Friday

This week I learned...

Use the space below to draw a picture or write about what you learned this week from your time in God's Word.

Week 5

Prayer focus for this week: Spend time praying for missionaries.

	Praying	Praise
Monday		
Tuesday		
Wednesday		
Thursday		
Friday		

BE KIND TO ONE ANOTHER, TENDERHEARTED, FORGIVING ONE ANOTHER, AS GOD IN CHRIST FORGAVE YOU.

Ephesians 4:32 (ESV)

Scripture for Week 5

DAVID THE FRIEND

MONDAY *1 SAMUEL 18:1-5 (ESV)*

¹⁸ As soon as he had finished speaking to Saul, the soul of Jonathan was knit to the soul of David, and Jonathan loved him as his own soul. ² And Saul took him that day and would not let him return to his father's house. ³ Then Jonathan made a covenant with David, because he loved him as his own soul. ⁴ And Jonathan stripped himself of the robe that was on him and gave it to David, and his armor, and even his sword and his bow and his belt. ⁵ And David went out and was successful wherever Saul sent him, so that Saul set him over the men of war. And this was good in the sight of all the people and also in the sight of Saul's servants.

1 SAMUEL 20:42 (ESV)

⁴² Then Jonathan said to David, "Go in peace, because we have sworn both of us in the name of the Lord, saying, 'The Lord shall be between me and you, and between my offspring and your offspring, forever.'" And he rose and departed, and Jonathan went into the city.

1 SAMUEL 23:16-18 (ESV)

¹⁶ And Jonathan, Saul's son, rose and went to David at Horesh, and strengthened his hand in God. ¹⁷ And he said to him, "Do not fear, for the hand of Saul my father shall not find you. You shall be king over Israel, and I shall be next to you. Saul my father also knows this." ¹⁸ And the two of them made a covenant before the Lord. David remained at Horesh, and Jonathan went home.

TUESDAY *2 SAMUEL 1:1-27 (ESV)*

¹ After the death of Saul, when David had returned from striking down the Amalekites, David remained two days in Ziklag. ² And on the third day, behold, a man came from Saul's camp, with his clothes torn and dirt on his head. And when he came to David, he fell to the ground and paid homage. ³ David said to him, "Where do you come from?" And he said to him, "I have escaped from the camp of Israel." ⁴ And David said to him, "How did it go? Tell me." And he answered, "The people fled from the battle, and also many of the people have fallen and are dead, and Saul and his son Jonathan are also dead."⁵ Then David said to the young man who told him, "How do

you know that Saul and his son Jonathan are dead?" ⁶ And the young man who told him said, "By chance I happened to be on Mount Gilboa, and there was Saul leaning on his spear, and behold, the chariots and the horsemen were close upon him. ⁷ And when he looked behind him, he saw me, and called to me. And I answered, 'Here I am.' ⁸ And he said to me, 'Who are you?' I answered him, 'I am an Amalekite.' ⁹ And he said to me, 'Stand beside me and kill me, for anguish has seized me, and yet my life still lingers.' ¹⁰ So I stood beside him and killed him, because I was sure that he could not live after he had fallen. And I took the crown that was on his head and the armlet that was on his arm, and I have brought them here to my lord."

¹¹ Then David took hold of his clothes and tore them, and so did all the men who were with him. ¹² And they mourned and wept and fasted until evening for Saul and for Jonathan his son and for the people of the Lord and for the house of Israel, because they had fallen by the sword. ¹³ And David said to the young man who told him, "Where do you come from?" And he answered, "I am the son of a sojourner, an Amalekite." ¹⁴ David said to him, "How is it you were not afraid to put out your hand to destroy the Lord's anointed?" ¹⁵ Then David called one of the young men and said, "Go, execute him." And he struck him down so that he died. ¹⁶ And David said to him, "Your blood be on your head, for your own mouth has testified against you, saying, 'I have killed the Lord's anointed.'"

¹⁷ And David lamented with this lamentation over Saul and Jonathan his son, ¹⁸ and he said it should be taught to the people of Judah; behold, it is written in the Book of Jashar. He said:

¹⁹ "Your glory, O Israel, is slain on your high places!
   How the mighty have fallen!
²⁰ Tell it not in Gath,
   publish it not in the streets of Ashkelon,
lest the daughters of the Philistines rejoice,
   lest the daughters of the uncircumcised exult.
²¹ "You mountains of Gilboa,
   let there be no dew or rain upon you,
   nor fields of offerings!
For there the shield of the mighty was defiled,
   the shield of Saul, not anointed with oil.
²² "From the blood of the slain,
   from the fat of the mighty,

the bow of Jonathan turned not back,

and the sword of Saul returned not empty.

[23] "Saul and Jonathan, beloved and lovely!

In life and in death they were not divided;

they were swifter than eagles;

they were stronger than lions.

[24] "You daughters of Israel, weep over Saul,

who clothed you luxuriously in scarlet,

who put ornaments of gold on your apparel.

[25] "How the mighty have fallen

in the midst of the battle!

"Jonathan lies slain on your high places.

[26]   I am distressed for you, my brother Jonathan;

very pleasant have you been to me;

your love to me was extraordinary,

surpassing the love of women.

[27] "How the mighty have fallen,

and the weapons of war perished!"

WEDNESDAY - JESUS THE BEST FRIEND   *JOHN 15:13-17 (ESV)*

[13] Greater love has no one than this, that someone lay down his life for his friends. [14] You are my friends if you do what I command you. [15] No longer do I call you servants, for the servant does not know what his master is doing; but I have called you friends, for all that I have heard from my Father I have made known to you. [16] You did not choose me, but I chose you and appointed you that you should go and bear fruit and that your fruit should abide, so that whatever you ask the Father in my name, he may give it to you. [17] These things I command you, so that you will love one another.

THURSDAY

PROVERBS 17:17 (ESV)

¹⁷ A friend loves at all times,

and a brother is born for adversity.

PROVERBS 18:24 (ESV)

A man of many companions may come to ruin,

but there is a friend who sticks closer than a brother.

FRIDAY

EPHESIANS 4:29-32 (ESV)

²⁹ Let no corrupting talk come out of your mouths, but only such as is good for building up, as fits the occasion, that it may give grace to those who hear. ³⁰ And do not grieve the Holy Spirit of God, by whom you were sealed for the day of redemption. ³¹ Let all bitterness and wrath and anger and clamor and slander be put away from you, along with all malice. ³² Be kind to one another, tenderhearted, forgiving one another, as God in Christ forgave you.

Monday

READ: 1 Samuel 18:1-5; 20:42; 23:16-18   WRITE: 1 Samuel 20:42

1. Write out today's **SCRIPTURE** passage.

_____

_____

_____

_____

_____

_____

_____

_____

_____

2. On the blank page to the right, **DRAW** or **WRITE** what this passage means to you.

3. My **PRAYER** for today:

_____

_____

_____

_____

_____

Monday

Tuesday

READ: 2 Samuel 1:1-27   **WRITE:** 2 Samuel 1:26

1. Write out today's **SCRIPTURE** passage.

_____

_____

_____

_____

_____

_____

_____

_____

_____

_____

2. On the blank page to the right, **DRAW** or **WRITE** what this passage means to you.

3. My **PRAYER** for today:

_____

_____

_____

_____

_____

_____

Tuesday

Wednesday

READ: John 15:13-17   WRITE: John 15:15

1. Write out today's **SCRIPTURE** passage.

_____

_____

_____

_____

_____

_____

_____

_____

_____

2. On the blank page to the right, **DRAW** or **WRITE** what this passage means to you.

3. My **PRAYER** for today:

_____

_____

_____

_____

_____

Wednesday

Thursday

READ: Proverbs 17:17; 18:24   **WRITE:** Proverbs 17:17

1. Write out today's **SCRIPTURE** passage.

_____

_____

_____

_____

_____

_____

_____

_____

_____

_____

2. On the blank page to the right, **DRAW** or **WRITE** what this passage means to you.

3. My **PRAYER** for today:

_____

_____

_____

_____

_____

Thursday

READ: Ephesians 4:29-32   WRITE: Ephesians 4:32

1. Write out today's **SCRIPTURE** passage.

_____

_____

_____

_____

_____

_____

_____

_____

_____

2. On the blank page to the right, **DRAW** or **WRITE** what this passage means to you.

3. My **PRAYER** for today:

_____

_____

_____

_____

_____

Friday

This week I learned...

Use the space below to draw a picture or write about what you learned this week from your time in God's Word.

Week 6

Prayer focus for this week: Spend time praying for you.

	Praying	Praise
Monday		
Tuesday		
Wednesday		
Thursday		
Friday		

REPENT

THEREFORE,

AND TURN BACK,

THAT YOUR SINS

MAY BE

BLOTTED

OUT.

Acts 3:19 (ESV)

Scripture for Week 6

WEEK 6 DAVID THE SINNER

MONDAY *2 SAMUEL 11:1–27 (ESV)*

¹¹ In the spring of the year, the time when kings go out to battle, David sent Joab, and his servants with him, and all Israel. And they ravaged the Ammonites and besieged Rabbah. But David remained at Jerusalem.

² It happened, late one afternoon, when David arose from his couch and was walking on the roof of the king's house, that he saw from the roof a woman bathing; and the woman was very beautiful. ³ And David sent and inquired about the woman. And one said, "Is not this Bathsheba, the daughter of Eliam, the wife of Uriah the Hittite?" ⁴ So David sent messengers and took her, and she came to him, and he lay with her. (Now she had been purifying herself from her uncleanness.) Then she returned to her house. ⁵ And the woman conceived, and she sent and told David, "I am pregnant."

⁶ So David sent word to Joab, "Send me Uriah the Hittite." And Joab sent Uriah to David.⁷ When Uriah came to him, David asked how Joab was doing and how the people were doing and how the war was going. ⁸ Then David said to Uriah, "Go down to your house and wash your feet." And Uriah went out of the king's house, and there followed him a present from the king. ⁹ But Uriah slept at the door of the king's house with all the servants of his lord, and did not go down to his house. ¹⁰ When they told David, "Uriah did not go down to his house," David said to Uriah, "Have you not come from a journey? Why did you not go down to your house?" ¹¹ Uriah said to David, "The ark and Israel and Judah dwell in booths, and my lord Joab and the servants of my lord are camping in the open field. Shall I then go to my house, to eat and to drink and to lie with my wife? As you live, and as your soul lives, I will not do this thing." ¹² Then David said to Uriah, "Remain here today also, and tomorrow I will send you back." So Uriah remained in Jerusalem that day and the next. ¹³ And David invited him, and he ate in his presence and drank, so that he made him drunk. And in the evening he went out to lie on his couch with the servants of his lord, but he did not go down to his house.

¹⁴ In the morning David wrote a letter to Joab and sent it by the hand of Uriah. ¹⁵ In the letter he wrote, "Set Uriah in the forefront of the hardest fighting, and then draw back from him, that he may be struck down, and die." ¹⁶ And as Joab was besieging the city, he assigned Uriah to the place where he knew there were valiant men. ¹⁷ And the men of the city came out and fought with Joab,

and some of the servants of David among the people fell. Uriah the Hittite also died. [18] Then Joab sent and told David all the news about the fighting. [19] And he instructed the messenger, "When you have finished telling all the news about the fighting to the king, [20] then, if the king's anger rises, and if he says to you, 'Why did you go so near the city to fight? Did you not know that they would shoot from the wall? [21] Who killed Abimelech the son of Jerubbesheth? Did not a woman cast an upper millstone on him from the wall, so that he died at Thebez? Why did you go so near the wall?' then you shall say, 'Your servant Uriah the Hittite is dead also.'"

[22] So the messenger went and came and told David all that Joab had sent him to tell. [23] The messenger said to David, "The men gained an advantage over us and came out against us in the field, but we drove them back to the entrance of the gate. [24] Then the archers shot at your servants from the wall. Some of the king's servants are dead, and your servant Uriah the Hittite is dead also." [25] David said to the messenger, "Thus shall you say to Joab, 'Do not let this matter displease you, for the sword devours now one and now another. Strengthen your attack against the city and overthrow it.' And encourage him."

[26] When the wife of Uriah heard that Uriah her husband was dead, she lamented over her husband. [27] And when the mourning was over, David sent and brought her to his house, and she became his wife and bore him a son. But the thing that David had done displeased the Lord.

TUESDAY   *2 SAMUEL 12:1–15 (ESV)*

[12] And the Lord sent Nathan to David. He came to him and said to him, "There were two men in a certain city, the one rich and the other poor. [2] The rich man had very many flocks and herds, [3] but the poor man had nothing but one little ewe lamb, which he had bought. And he brought it up, and it grew up with him and with his children. It used to eat of his morsel and drink from his cup and lie in his arms, and it was like a daughter to him. [4] Now there came a traveler to the rich man, and he was unwilling to take one of his own flock or herd to prepare for the guest who had come to him, but he took the poor man's lamb and prepared it for the man who had come to him." [5] Then David's anger was greatly kindled against the man, and he said to Nathan, "As the Lord lives, the man who has done this deserves to die, [6] and he shall restore the lamb fourfold, because he did this thing, and because he had no pity."

[7] Nathan said to David, "You are the man! Thus says the Lord, the God of Israel, 'I anointed you king over Israel, and I delivered you out of the hand of Saul. [8] And I gave you your master's house

and your master's wives into your arms and gave you the house of Israel and of Judah. And if this were too little, I would add to you as much more. ⁹ Why have you despised the word of the Lord, to do what is evil in his sight? You have struck down Uriah the Hittite with the sword and have taken his wife to be your wife and have killed him with the sword of the Ammonites. ¹⁰ Now therefore the sword shall never depart from your house, because you have despised me and have taken the wife of Uriah the Hittite to be your wife.' ¹¹ Thus says the Lord, 'Behold, I will raise up evil against you out of your own house. And I will take your wives before your eyes and give them to your neighbor, and he shall lie with your wives in the sight of this sun. ¹² For you did it secretly, but I will do this thing before all Israel and before the sun.'" ¹³ David said to Nathan, "I have sinned against the Lord." And Nathan said to David, "The Lord also has put away your sin; you shall not die. ¹⁴ Nevertheless, because by this deed you have utterly scorned the Lord, the child who is born to you shall die." ¹⁵ Then Nathan went to his house.

And the Lord afflicted the child that Uriah's wife bore to David, and he became sick.

WEDNESDAY - JESUS, THE HOPE OF SINNER   *1 TIMOTHY 1:12-16 (ESV)*

¹² I thank him who has given me strength, Christ Jesus our Lord, because he judged me faithful, appointing me to his service, ¹³ though formerly I was a blasphemer, persecutor, and insolent opponent. But I received mercy because I had acted ignorantly in unbelief,¹⁴ and the grace of our Lord overflowed for me with the faith and love that are in Christ Jesus. ¹⁵ The saying is trustworthy and deserving of full acceptance, that Christ Jesus came into the world to save sinners, of whom I am the foremost. ¹⁶ But I received mercy for this reason, that in me, as the foremost, Jesus Christ might display his perfect patience as an example to those who were to believe in him for eternal life.

THURSDAY

²¹ And when the Lord smelled the pleasing aroma, the Lord said in his heart, "I will never again curse the ground because of man, for the intention of man's heart is evil from his youth. Neither will I ever again strike down every living creature as I have done.

1 JOHN 1:8-9 (ESV)

⁸ If we say we have no sin, we deceive ourselves, and the truth is not in us. ⁹ If we confess our sins, he is faithful and just to forgive us our sins and to cleanse us from all unrighteousness.

FRIDAY

1ACTS 3:19 (ESV)

⁹ Repent therefore, and turn back, that your sins may be blotted out

Monday

READ: 2 Samuel 11:1–27   **WRITE:** 2 Samuel 11:27

1. Write out today's **SCRIPTURE** passage.

_____

_____

_____

_____

_____

_____

_____

_____

_____

_____

2. On the blank page to the right, **DRAW** or **WRITE** what this passage means to you.

3. My **PRAYER** for today:

_____

_____

_____

_____

_____

Monday

Tuesday

READ: 2 Samuel 12:1–15   **WRITE:** 2 Samuel 12:13-15

1. Write out today's **SCRIPTURE** passage.

_____

_____

_____

_____

_____

_____

_____

_____

_____

_____

2. On the blank page to the right, **DRAW** or **WRITE** what this passage means to you.

3. My **PRAYER** for today:

_____

_____

_____

_____

_____

_____

Tuesday

Wednesday

READ: 1 Timothy 1:12-16

WRITE: 1 Timothy 1:15

1. Write out today's **SCRIPTURE** passage.

_____

_____

_____

_____

_____

_____

_____

_____

_____

_____

2. On the blank page to the right, **DRAW** or **WRITE** what this passage means to you.

3. My **PRAYER** for today:

_____

_____

_____

_____

_____

Wednesday

Thursday

READ: Genesis 8:21; 1 John 1:8-9   **WRITE**: 1 John 1:8-9

1. Write out today's **SCRIPTURE** passage.

_____

_____

_____

_____

_____

_____

_____

_____

_____

2. On the blank page to the right, **DRAW** or **WRITE** what this passage means to you.

3. My **PRAYER** for today:

_____

_____

_____

_____

_____

Thursday

Friday

READ: Acts 3:19   **WRITE:** Acts 3:19

1. Write out today's **SCRIPTURE** passage.

_____

_____

_____

_____

_____

_____

_____

2. On the blank page to the right, **DRAW** or **WRITE** what this passage means to you.

3. My **PRAYER** for today:

_____

_____

_____

_____

Friday

This week I learned...

Use the space below to draw a picture or write about what you learned this week from your time in God's Word.

Week 7

Prayer focus for this week: Spend time turning your fears into prayers.

	Praying	Praise
Monday		
Tuesday		
Wednesday		
Thursday		
Friday		

BUT YOU ARE A CHOSEN RACE, A ROYAL PRIESTHOOD, A HOLY NATION, A PEOPLE FOR HIS OWN POSSESSION, THAT YOU MAY PROCLAIM THE EXCELLENCIES OF HIM WHO CALLED YOU OUT OF DARKNESS INTO HIS MARVELOUS LIGHT.

1 Peter 2:9 (ESV)

Scripture for Week 7

DAVID THE MAN AFTER GOD'S HEART

MONDAY   *ACTS 13:22 (ESV)*

²² And when he had removed him, he raised up David to be their king, of whom he testified and said, 'I have found in David the son of Jesse a man after my heart, who will do all my will.'

TUESDAY   *1 SAMUEL 13: 8-15 (ESV)*

⁸ He waited seven days, the time appointed by Samuel. But Samuel did not come to Gilgal, and the people were scattering from him. ⁹ So Saul said, "Bring the burnt offering here to me, and the peace offerings." And he offered the burnt offering. ¹⁰ As soon as he had finished offering the burnt offering, behold, Samuel came. And Saul went out to meet him and greet him. ¹¹ Samuel said, "What have you done?" And Saul said, "When I saw that the people were scattering from me, and that you did not come within the days appointed, and that the Philistines had mustered at Michmash, ¹² I said, 'Now the Philistines will come down against me at Gilgal, and I have not sought the favor of the Lord.' So I forced myself, and offered the burnt offering." ¹³ And Samuel said to Saul, "You have done foolishly. You have not kept the command of the Lord your God, with which he commanded you. For then the Lord would have established your kingdom over Israel forever. ¹⁴ But now your kingdom shall not continue. The Lord has sought out a man after his own heart, and the Lord has commanded him to be prince[a] over his people, because you have not kept what the Lord commanded you." ¹⁵ And Samuel arose and went up from Gilgal. The rest of the people went up after Saul to meet the army; they went up from Gilgal[b] to Gibeah of Benjamin.

And Saul numbered the people who were present with him, about six hundred men.

WEDNESDAY - JESUS BELOVED OF GOD   *MATTHEW 17:1-7 (ESV)*

17 And after six days Jesus took with him Peter and James, and John his brother, and led them up a high mountain by themselves. 2 And he was transfigured before them, and his face shone like the sun, and his clothes became white as light. 3 And behold, there appeared to them Moses and Elijah, talking with him. 4 And Peter said to Jesus, "Lord, it is good that we are here. If you wish, I will make three tents here, one for you and one for Moses and one for Elijah." 5 He was still speaking when, behold, a bright cloud overshadowed them, and a voice from the cloud said, "This is my beloved Son, with whom I am well pleased; listen to him." 6 When the disciples heard this, they fell on their faces and were terrified. 7 But Jesus came and touched them, saying, "Rise, and have no fear."

THURSDAY   *MATTHEW 10:29-31 (ESV)*

29 Are not two sparrows sold for a penny? And not one of them will fall to the ground apart from your Father. 30 But even the hairs of your head are all numbered. 31 Fear not, therefore; you are of more value than many sparrows.

FRIDAY   *1 PETER 2:9-10 (ESV)*

9 But you are a chosen race, a royal priesthood, a holy nation, a people for his own possession, that you may proclaim the excellencies of him who called you out of darkness into his marvelous light. 10 Once you were not a people, but now you are God's people; once you had not received mercy, but now you have received mercy.

Monday

READ: Acts 13:22

WRITE: Acts 13:22

1. Write out today's **SCRIPTURE** passage.

_____

_____

_____

_____

_____

_____

_____

_____

_____

_____

2. On the blank page to the right, **DRAW** or **WRITE** what this passage means to you.

3. My **PRAYER** for today:

_____

_____

_____

_____

_____

Monday

Tuesday

READ: 1 Samuel 13: 8-15   **WRITE:** 1 Samuel 13:14

1. Write out today's **SCRIPTURE** passage.

_____

_____

_____

_____

_____

_____

_____

_____

_____

2. On the blank page to the right, **DRAW** or **WRITE** what this passage means to you.

3. My **PRAYER** for today:

_____

_____

_____

_____

_____

Tuesday

Wednesday

READ: Matthew 17:1-7   WRITE: Matthew 17:5

1. Write out today's SCRIPTURE passage.

_____

_____

_____

_____

_____

_____

_____

_____

_____

2. On the blank page to the right, DRAW or WRITE what this passage means to you.

3. My PRAYER for today:

_____

_____

_____

_____

_____

Wednesday

READ: Matthew 10:29-31   WRITE: Matthew 10:29-31

1. Write out today's **SCRIPTURE** passage.

_____

_____

_____

_____

_____

_____

_____

_____

_____

_____

2. On the blank page to the right, **DRAW** or **WRITE** what this passage means to you.

3. My **PRAYER** for today:

_____

_____

_____

_____

_____

_____

Thursday

Friday

READ: 1 Peter 2:9-10　　　　　　　　**WRITE**: 1 Peter 2:9

1. Write out today's **SCRIPTURE** passage.

_____

_____

_____

_____

_____

_____

_____

_____

_____

_____

2. On the blank page to the right, **DRAW** or **WRITE** what this passage means to you.

3. My **PRAYER** for today:

_____

_____

_____

_____

_____

_____

Friday

This week I learned...

Use the space below to draw a picture or write about what you learned this week from your time in God's Word.

Week 8

Prayer focus for this week: Spend time thanking God for how he is working in your life.

	Praying	Praise
Monday		
Tuesday		
Wednesday		
Thursday		
Friday		

BUT THE LORD IS FAITHFUL. HE WILL ESTABLISH YOU AND GUARD YOU AGAINST THE EVIL ONE.

2 Thessalonians 3:3 (ESV)

Scripture for Week 8

DAVID A MAN OF FAITH

MONDAY   *1 SAMUEL 17:33-47 (ESV)*

³³ And Saul said to David, "You are not able to go against this Philistine to fight with him, for you are but a youth, and he has been a man of war from his youth." ³⁴ But David said to Saul, "Your servant used to keep sheep for his father. And when there came a lion, or a bear, and took a lamb from the flock, ³⁵ I went after him and struck him and delivered it out of his mouth. And if he arose against me, I caught him by his beard and struck him and killed him. ³⁶ Your servant has struck down both lions and bears, and this uncircumcised Philistine shall be like one of them, for he has defied the armies of the living God." ³⁷ And David said, "The Lord who delivered me from the paw of the lion and from the paw of the bear will deliver me from the hand of this Philistine." And Saul said to David, "Go, and the Lord be with you!"

³⁸ Then Saul clothed David with his armor. He put a helmet of bronze on his head and clothed him with a coat of mail, ³⁹ and David strapped his sword over his armor. And he tried in vain to go, for he had not tested them. Then David said to Saul, "I cannot go with these, for I have not tested them." So David put them off. ⁴⁰ Then he took his staff in his hand and chose five smooth stones from the brook and put them in his shepherd's pouch. His sling was in his hand, and he approached the Philistine.

⁴¹ And the Philistine moved forward and came near to David, with his shield-bearer in front of him. ⁴² And when the Philistine looked and saw David, he disdained him, for he was but a youth, ruddy and handsome in appearance. ⁴³ And the Philistine said to David, "Am I a dog, that you come to me with sticks?" And the Philistine cursed David by his gods. ⁴⁴ The Philistine said to David, "Come to me, and I will give your flesh to the birds of the air and to the beasts of the field." ⁴⁵ Then David said to the Philistine, "You come to me with a sword and with a spear and with a javelin, but I come to you in the name of theLord of hosts, the God of the armies of Israel, whom you have defied. ⁴⁶ This day the Lordwill deliver you into my hand, and I will strike you down and cut off your head. And I will give the dead bodies of the host of the Philistines this day to the birds of the air and to the wild beasts of the earth, that all the earth may know that there is a God in Israel, ⁴⁷ and that all this assembly may know that the Lord saves not with sword and spear. For the battle is the Lord's, and he will give you into our hand."

The Lord is my light and my salvation;

    whom shall I fear?

The Lord is the stronghold of my life;

    of whom shall I be afraid?

[2] When evildoers assail me

    to eat up my flesh,

my adversaries and foes,

    it is they who stumble and fall.

[3] Though an army encamp against me,

    my heart shall not fear;

though war arise against me,

    yet I will be confident.

[4] One thing have I asked of the Lord,

    that will I seek after:

that I may dwell in the house of the Lord

    all the days of my life,

to gaze upon the beauty of the Lord

    and to inquire in his temple.

[5] For he will hide me in his shelter

    in the day of trouble;

he will conceal me under the cover of his tent;

    he will lift me high upon a rock.

[6] And now my head shall be lifted up

    above my enemies all around me,

and I will offer in his tent

    sacrifices with shouts of joy;

I will sing and make melody to the Lord.

[7] Hear, O Lord, when I cry aloud;

    be gracious to me and answer me!

[8] You have said, "Seek my face."

My heart says to you,

    "Your face, Lord, do I seek."

[9]   Hide not your face from me.

Turn not your servant away in anger,

O you who have been my help.

Cast me not off; forsake me not,

    O God of my salvation!

[10] For my father and my mother have forsaken me,

    but the Lord will take me in.

[11] Teach me your way, O Lord,

    and lead me on a level path

    because of my enemies.

[12] Give me not up to the will of my adversaries;

    for false witnesses have risen against me,

    and they breathe out violence.

[13] I believe that I shall look upon the goodness of the Lord

    in the land of the living!

[14] Wait for the Lord;

    be strong, and let your heart take courage;

    wait for the Lord!

WEDNESDAY - JESUS IS FAITHFUL   *2 THESSALONIANS 3:1-5 (ESV)*

[3] Finally, brothers, pray for us, that the word of the Lord may speed ahead and be honored, as happened among you, [2] and that we may be delivered from wicked and evil men. For not all have faith. [3] But the Lord is faithful. He will establish you and guard you against the evil one. [4] And we have confidence in the Lord about you, that you are doing and will do the things that we command. [5] May the Lord direct your hearts to the love of God and to the steadfastness of Christ.

THURSDAY

JEREMIAH 17:7-8 (ESV)

7 "Blessed is the man who trusts in the Lord,

    whose trust is the Lord.

8 He is like a tree planted by water,

    that sends out its roots by the stream,

and does not fear when heat comes,

    for its leaves remain green,

and is not anxious in the year of drought,

    for it does not cease to bear fruit."

FRIDAY

HEBREWS 10:19-25 (ESV)

19 Therefore, brothers, since we have confidence to enter the holy places by the blood of Jesus, 20 by the new and living way that he opened for us through the curtain, that is, through his flesh, 21 and since we have a great priest over the house of God, 22 let us draw near with a true heart in full assurance of faith, with our hearts sprinkled clean from an evil conscience and our bodies washed with pure water. 23 Let us hold fast the confession of our hope without wavering, for he who promised is faithful. 24 And let us consider how to stir up one another to love and good works, 25 not neglecting to meet together, as is the habit of some, but encouraging one another, and all the more as you see the Day drawing near.

Monday

READ: 1 Samuel 17:33-47   WRITE: 1 Samuel 17:45

1. Write out today's SCRIPTURE passage.

_____

_____

_____

_____

_____

_____

_____

_____

_____

2. On the blank page to the right, DRAW or WRITE what this passage means to you.

3. My PRAYER for today:

_____

_____

_____

_____

_____

Monday

Tuesday

READ: Psalm 27   **WRITE**: Psalm 27:1

1. Write out today's **SCRIPTURE** passage.

_____

_____

_____

_____

_____

_____

_____

_____

_____

2. On the blank page to the right, **DRAW** or **WRITE** what this passage means to you.

3. My **PRAYER** for today:

_____

_____

_____

_____

_____

Tuesday

Wednesday

READ: 2 Thessalonians 3:1-5   WRITE: 2 Thessalonians 3:3-5

1. Write out today's **SCRIPTURE** passage.

_____

_____

_____

_____

_____

_____

_____

_____

_____

_____

2. On the blank page to the right, **DRAW** or **WRITE** what this passage means to you.

3. My **PRAYER** for today:

_____

_____

_____

_____

_____

Wednesday

Thursday

READ: Jeremiah 17:7-8   **WRITE**: Jeremiah 17:7-8

1. Write out today's **SCRIPTURE** passage.

_____

_____

_____

_____

_____

_____

_____

_____

_____

2. On the blank page to the right, **DRAW** or **WRITE** what this passage means to you.

3. My **PRAYER** for today:

_____

_____

_____

_____

_____

Thursday

Friday

1. Write out today's **SCRIPTURE** passage.

_____

_____

_____

_____

_____

_____

_____

_____

_____

2. On the blank page to the right, **DRAW** or **WRITE** what this passage means to you.

3. My **PRAYER** for today:

_____

_____

_____

_____

_____

_____

Friday

This week I learned...

Use the space below to draw a picture or write about what you learned this week from your time in God's Word.